The 4 Cuties – Freundinnen

The Spring Collection

Part VIII

For my husband

The nice 4 Cuties are in the land

and present

their new spring collection

a amazing selection

of Images with sun

and a lot of fun

for the next summer time

that is fine

Songs for the 4 Cuties

The Cutiesong

The 4 Cuties

are the best

friends yes

they running in the land

hand in hand

hand in hand

running in the land

the 4 cuties are the best

The new Cutiesong

Sing the Cutiesong

All time long

yes with yeppa say JAAA

Cuties on the world

singing a word

with the song

all time long

Sing the Cutiesong

All time long Yes with yeppa say
JAAA

Where are the cuties?

Beginning with one

3000 girls with fun

cuties everywhere

are there

Wo sind die Cuties

sie sind lucky

Everybody can do
what to do
in his own house

Wo sind die Cuties
sie sind lucky

Understanding or not
they are hot
all sisters by me
cuties I see

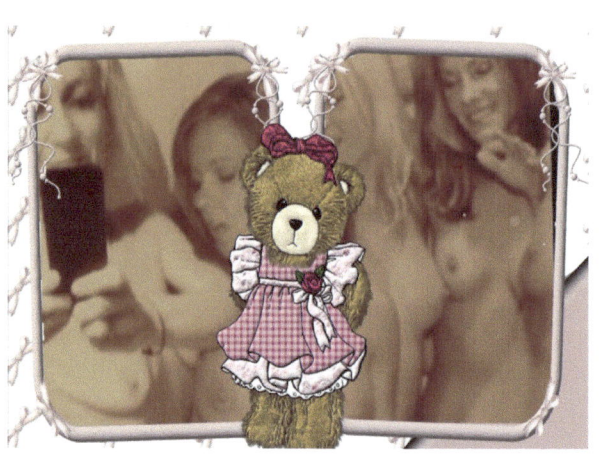

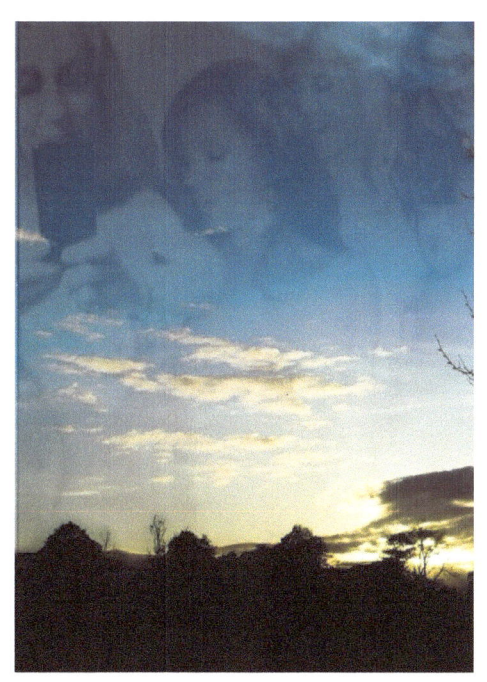

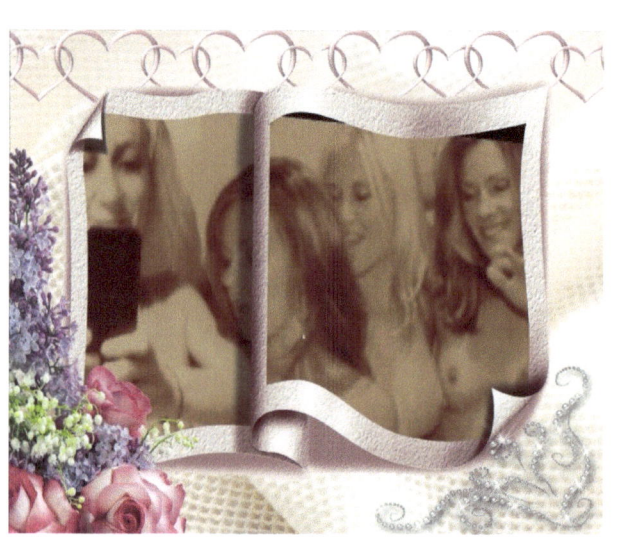

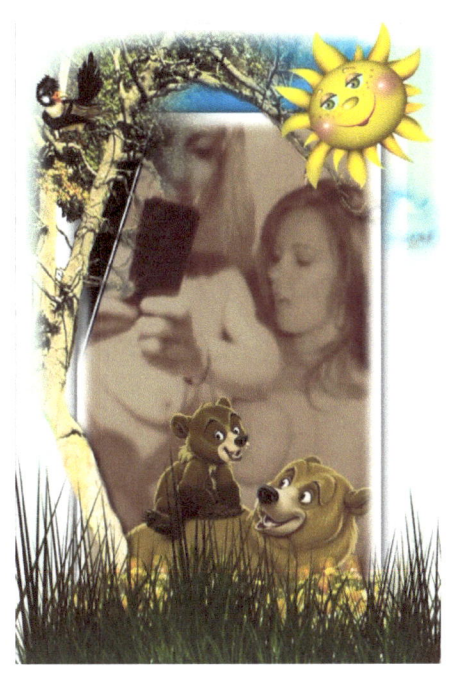

The 4 are the best girls — they are therapist, have their own

make — up collection, retroedition , diamantcollection and now the spring is coming. For the four Freundinnen — love is in the air, everywhere.

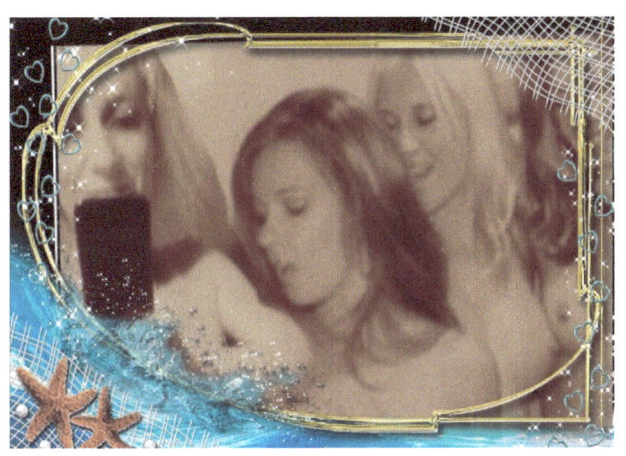

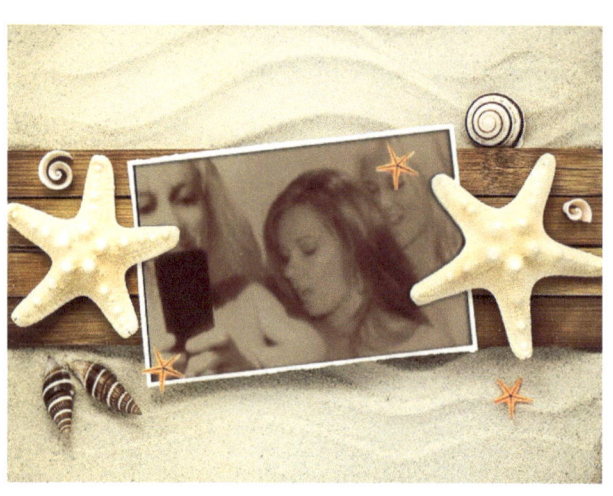

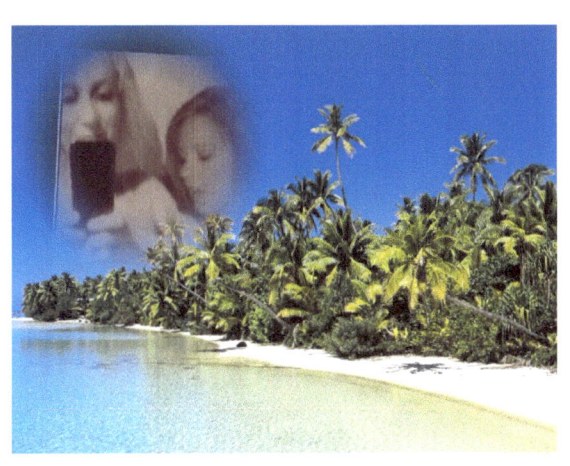

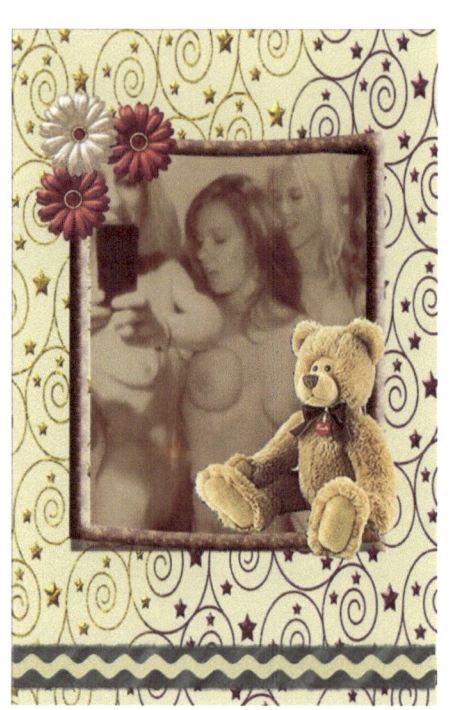

The first flowers - the girlfriends making pictures, photos, they have a passion: Collage with frames. That is no problem for them, they are looking for the best and go to work. Addicted to poetry – the poems, lyrics go hand in hand with the images.

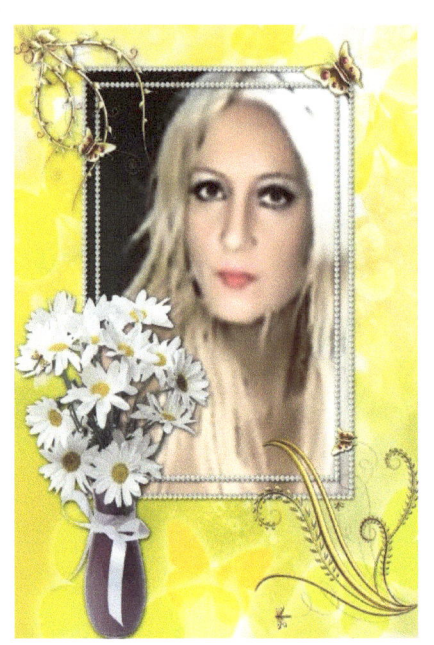

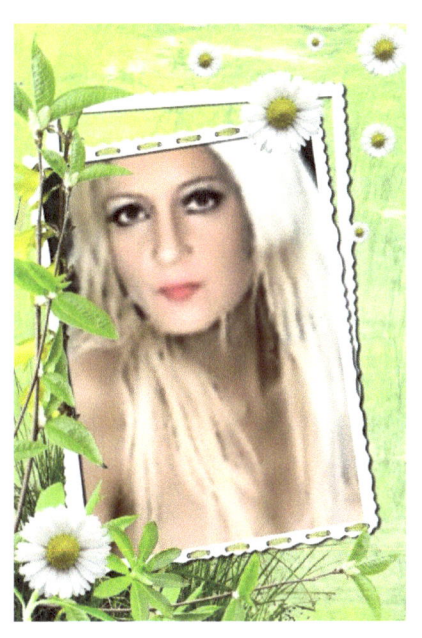

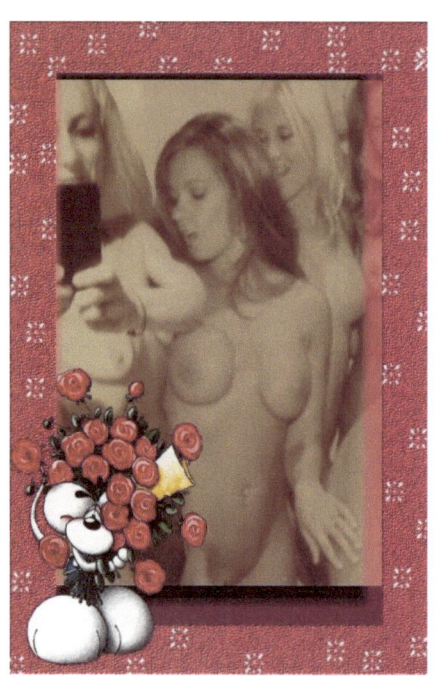

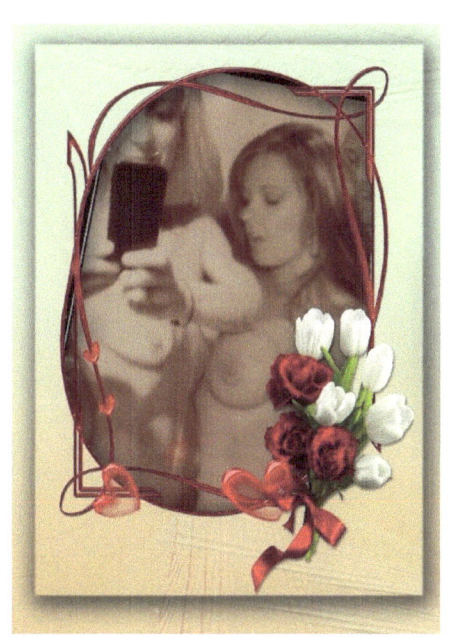

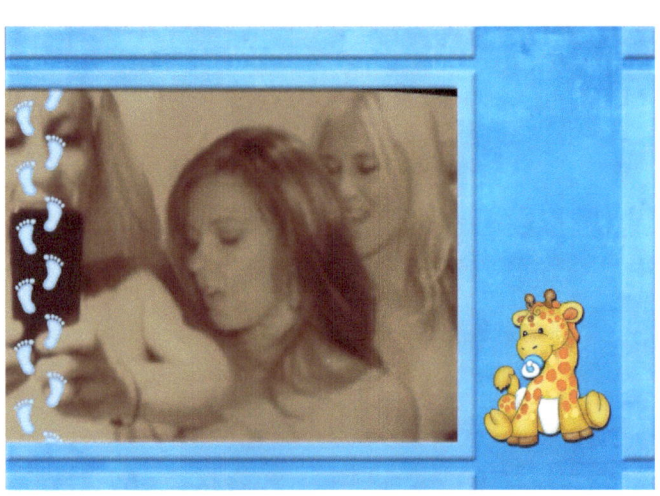

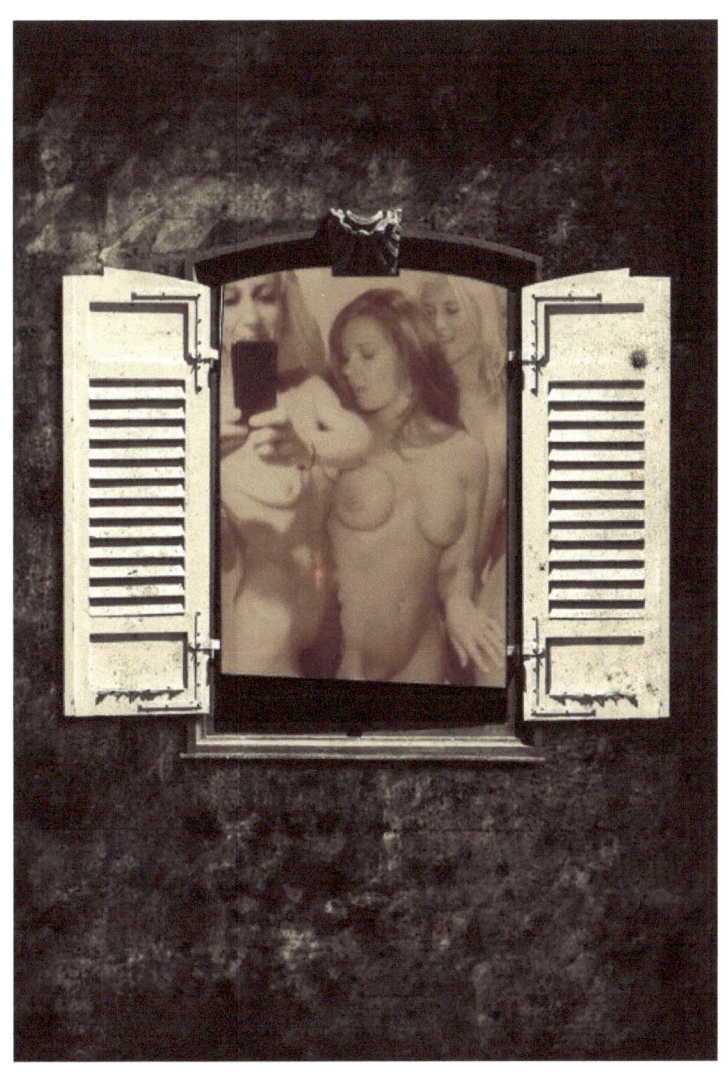

They have lust to use the make – up, their own collection. The mirror shows the beauty of the 4. First they take the foundation and the last step is the lipstick. Hot red, that the best colour for the spring – waiting of the summertime.

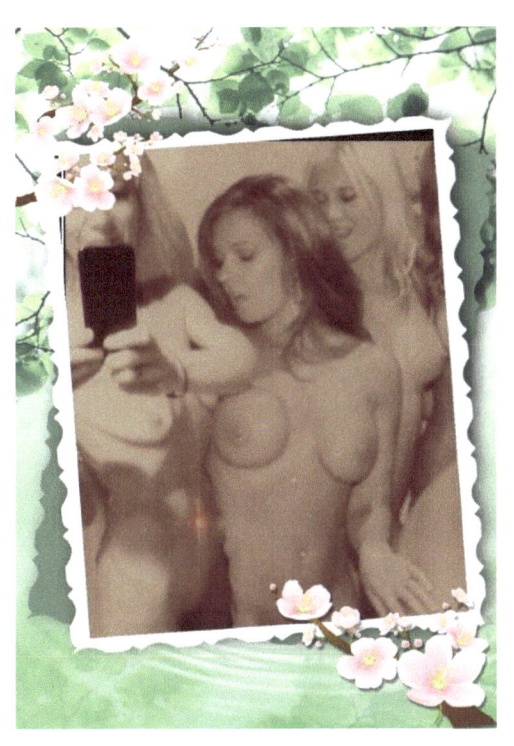

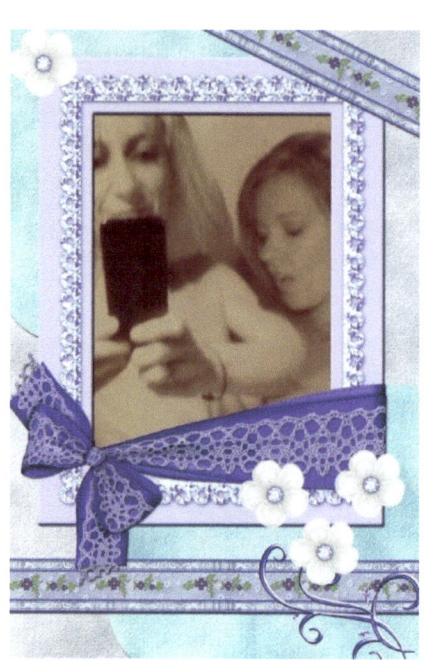

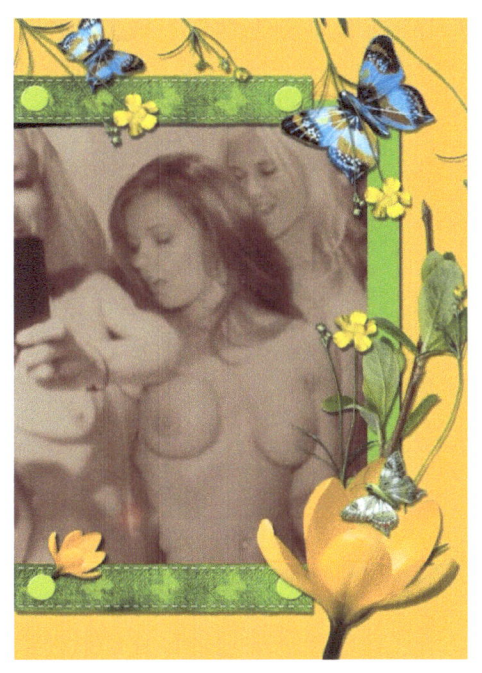

I say Thank you to my husband